SNOWBOARDING

BY HOLLIE ENDRES

BELLWETHER MEDIA · MINNEAPOLIS, MN

Are you ready to take it to the extreme?

Torque books thrust you into the action-packed world of sports, vehicles, and adventure. These books may include dirt, smoke, fire, and dangerous stunts.

WARNING: read at your own risk.

7/08

This edition first published in 2008 by Bellwether Media.

No part of this publication may be reproduced in whole or in part without written permission of the publisher. For information regarding permission, write to Bellwether Media Inc., Attention: Permissions Department, Post Office Box 1C, Minnetonka, MN 55345-9998.

Library of Congress Cataloging-in-Publication Data
Endres, Hollie J.
   Snowboarding / by Hollie J. Endres.
      p. cm. -- (Torque : action sports)
   Summary: "Photographs of amazing feats accompany engaging information about snowboarding. The combination of high-interest subject matter and light text is intended to engage readers in grades 3 through 7"--Provided by publisher.
   Includes bibliographical references and index.
   ISBN-13: 978-1-60014-128-7 (hardcover : alk. paper)
   ISBN-10: 1-60014-128-5 (hardcover : alk. paper)
   1. Snowboarding--Juvenile literature. I. Title.

   GV857.S57E53 2008
   796.939--dc22   2007019869

c-1

CONTENTS

RIDING THE SLOPE

Two snowboarders start down a mountain slope. Their boards kick up powdery snow as they weave back and forth. The snowboarders glide around trees and boulders. A cold wind blows across their faces.

The snowboarders come upon a steep drop-off. They tuck into crouching positions and leap into the air. They land gracefully at the bottom and continue their run down the mountain.

FaSt FaCt

Marco Siffredi of France
made history when he
became the first person
to ride Mt. Everest, the
world's tallest mountain,
on May 24th, 2001.

WHAT IS SNOWBOARDING?

Snowboarding is both a popular hobby and a serious sport. Most people snowboard on marked trails called **runs**. Snowboarders who like unmarked mountainsides are called **freeriders**. Some more serious riders enjoy competitive racing. Others do freestyle tricks off of jumps and in **half-pipes**.

Snowboarding has been around since the mid-1960s. Inventor Sherman Poppen created the first snowboard in 1965. He tied two snow skis together and added a rope to be used as a handle. Poppen combined the words "snow" and "surfer" and called it a **"snurfer."** Now snowboarding is popular around the world.

EQUIPMENT

Today's snowboards are made of wood and **fiberglass**. Most of them have metal edges for cutting through snow. **Bindings** attached to the top of the board hold the rider's feet firmly in place.

Bindings

There are three main styles of snowboards. Long and narrow alpine boards are built for speed. Freestyle boards are extremely short and very wide. They are the best snowboards for doing tricks. Freeride boards are a cross between freestyle and alpine boards.

IN ACTION

The two main kinds of snowboard racing are **slalom** and **Super G**. Slalom racers weave through a series of gates as they go down a slope. They try to make sharp turns without losing their balance. Super G racers go full-speed down a twisting course filled with jumps. As many as four riders jump, bump, and race their way to the finish line.

Freestyle competitions are packed with thrilling tricks. These competitions include the half-pipe and **big air** events. A half-pipe is a deep trench in the snow. Snowboarders cruise down the half-pipe moving from side to side doing tricks.

They do flips, spins, and board grabs to earn points. Snowboarders only get one jump in the big air event. They build up speed on a steep slope and hit a huge jump at the bottom. They sail into the air and do the biggest trick they can.

These events and some of today's biggest stars make snowboarding popular worldwide.

Shaun White celebrates another victory at the X Games.

GLOSSARY

big air—a snowboarding event where riders get one jump to do their best trick

binding—a set of straps that keep a snowboarder's feet attached to the board

fiberglass—a light and durable material made of woven glass fibers

freerider—a snowboarder who likes unmarked trails

half-pipe—a long, curved, snow-covered trench on which snowboarders do tricks

runs—marked snowboarding trails

slalom—a type of race in which snowboarders race between sets of gates

snurfer—the name for the earliest snowboards, combining the words "snow" with "surfer"

super g—a snowboarding race where riders speed down a slope

TO LEARN MORE

AT THE LIBRARY

Doeden, Matt. *Snowboarding*.
Mankato, Minn.: Capstone Press, 2005.

Doeden, Matt. *Shaun White*. Minneapolis, Minn.:
Lerner Publications, 2007.

Slade, Suzanne. *Let's Go Snowboarding!*
New York: PowerKids Press, 2007.

ON THE WEB

Learning more about snowboarding
is as easy as 1, 2, 3.

1. Go to www.factsurfer.com
2. Enter "snowboarding" into search box.
3. Click the "Surf" button and you will see a list
   of related web sites.

With factsurfer.com, finding more
information is just a click away.

INDEX